My Creations

My First Knitting Book

Easy-to-Follow Instructions and More Than 15 Projects

Hildegarde Deuzo

Dover Publications, Inc.
Mineola, New York

To my Granny, who let me rummage through the Oxi-Clean tub
where she kept her leftover yarn when I was a little girl.
H.D.

Bibliographical Note

My First Knitting Book: Easy-to-Follow Instructions and More Than 15 Projects,
first published by Dover Publications, Inc., in 2016, is a new English translation of
Premiers tricots, originally published by Fleurus Editions, Paris, in 2013.

Library of Congress Cataloging-in-Publication Data

Names: Deuzo, Hildegarde, author.
Title: My first knitting book : easy-to-follow instructions and more than 15
    projects / Hildegarde Deuzo.
Other titles: Premiers tricots. English
Description: Mineola, New York : Dover Publications, Inc, 2016. | Translation
    of: Premiers tricots.
Identifiers: LCCN 2016008012| ISBN 9780486805658 | ISBN 0486805654
Subjects: LCSH: Knitting.
Classification: LCC TT820 .D399513 2016 | DDC 746.43/2—dc23 LC record available
at http://lccn.loc.gov/2016008012

Manufactured in the United States by LSC Communications
80565402   2020
www.doverpublications.com

KEY TO KNITTING TERMS

BO	bind off
CO	cast on
K	knit
k2tog	knit 2 stitches together
LH	left hand
LS	left side
P	purl
p2tog	purl 2 stitches together
RH	right hand
RS	right side
SKP *or* sl, kl, psso	slip 1, knit 1, pass slipped stitch over
sts	stitches
tog	together
WS	wrong side

Materials

Contrary to what most people think, the basic knitting techniques are really easy. And once you master them, knitting is a fun and rewarding activity. Just imagine how proudly you will say: "I knitted it myself!"

The Needles

They are made of different materials and come in different sizes indicated by a number: the higher the number, the bigger the needle. The size of the needle you will use is dependent upon the thickness of the yarn your project calls for. For a beginner, needles from size 4 (3.5mm) to 8 (5mm) are perfect. Word to the wise: your first project should be manageable in size.

Depending on your particular knitting style, you may have to use needles one size larger or smaller than the pattern calls for.

The Yarn

The choices are many! At first, choose a plain—not fuzzy—yarn so you can easily see each stitch. Yarns with high contents of natural fibers (cotton or wool) are the most pleasant to work with.

The balls of yarn come wrapped in a band, which provides useful information: suggested needle size, weight and length of yarn in the ball, dye lot number and/or color number, washing instructions, number of stitches and rows for a 4" (10cm) square. When working on a project that uses several balls of yarn, it is important to work with the same dye lot number.

Other Materials

Crochet hook to attach tassels or fringe, and to pick up dropped stitches.

Jewelry pliers (see p. 52).

Pins to secure your pieces together.

Pointy scissors

Sewing needle and sewing thread

Tape measure, preferably in inches and centimeters.

Tapestry needle (also called yarn needle) to weave in the ends and sew pieces together.

Finishing touches: buttons, felt, studs, beads, etc.

Stitch counters can be purchased to help count the rows in your knitting. Alternatively, you can make a mark on a piece of paper each time you finish a row.

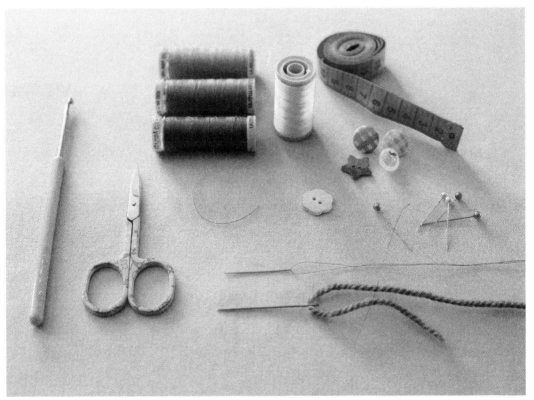

"How To" of Knitting

To learn how to knit, you just need a ball of yarn, knitting needles, and some patience! Most importantly, you need to explore what to do with your right hand (RH) and your left hand (LH). If you're a leftie, substitute left for "right" and right for "left" in the text, or look at the drawings in a mirror.

How to Hold Your Knitting Needles

Hold one needle in each hand between the thumb and index finger: hold the left needle rather close to its tip and the right needle a little further down. The other fingers are folded and help to secure each needle.

How to Hold the Yarn

Each knitter adopts the knitting style that feels most natural. Just remember that the RH has to gently hold the yarn without holding it too tightly or letting it fall off your fingers. The drawing shows the classical method: the index finger guides the yarn with total precision.

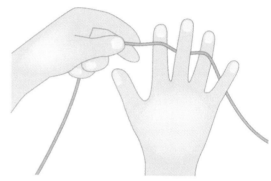

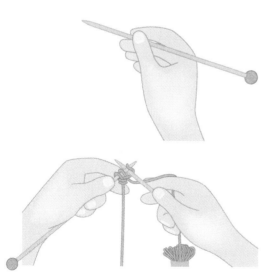

Those are the basics! Each of us has to determine the knitting style that feels most comfortable. One thing to remember: remain relaxed so that your hands don't become sore and your knitting stays supple and even.

To Begin

Knitting always starts by casting on, i.e. creating the first row of stitches. The first stitch is always a slip knot.

Slip Knot

1 Leaving about a 6" (15cm) tail of yarn, create a loose loop around the left index finger and hold it with the thumb.

2 Using the yarn attached to the ball instead of the tail, position the yarn above the loop.

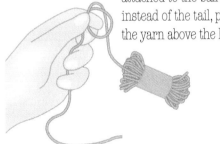

3 Pull this end of the yarn through the loop to obtain a new loop.

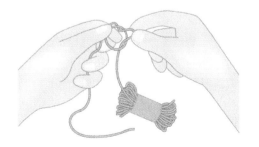

4 Holding the tail, gently pull to tighten the knot.

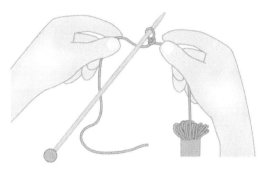

5 Insert the knitting needle into the loop. Gently pull on both ends of the yarn to make sure that the knot is tight enough.

Make yourself comfortable! You'll love knitting even more if you are seated comfortably and relaxed.

Casting On

There are several ways to cast on (CO). The one described below is simple and creates a supple edge.

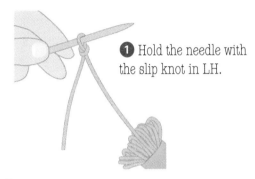

1 Hold the needle with the slip knot in LH.

2 From the front of the project—the side that people will see, or the Right Side (RS)—insert the RH needle in the loop under the LH needle.

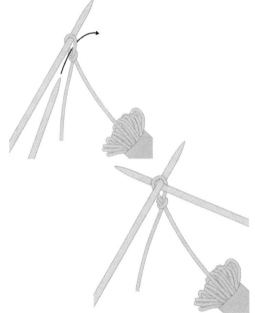

3 With the right hand, bring the yarn over the RH needle tip and tighten it a little to position it between the tips of the two needles.

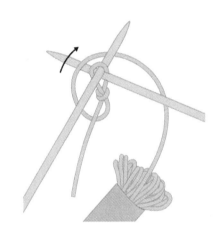

4 With the tip of the RH needle, bring the yarn toward you through the loop, creating a new loop on the RH needle.

5 Insert the tip of the LH needle in the new loop and pull out the RH needle. There are now two stitches on the LH needle. Gently tighten the new loop on the LH needle.

Be careful not to tighten the stitches too much; it will be easier to slide the RH needle between the last two stitches when the next stitch is cast on.

7 Bring the yarn toward you through the last stitch, so as to form a third stitch. Transfer this stitch to the LH needle and gently tighten it as you did with the previous stitch.

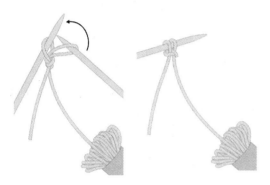

6 Insert the tip of the RH needle under the LH needle, between the two stitches. Pass the yarn over the tip of the RH needle, from left to right.

8 To cast on more stitches, repeat steps 6 and 7 until you have the number of stitches needed for your knitting project.

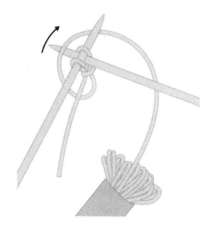

When pulling back the yarn to create a new stitch (steps 4 and 7), use the LH index finger to push and guide the RH needle.

11

The Knit Stitch

The knit stitch is the basic stitch of knitting and is the easiest to learn. This simple stitch will allow you to create many projects. When using the knit stitch on every row, you create a stitch pattern called garter stitch (see page 18).

1 Hold the needle with the cast on stitches in the LH. Insert the RH needle into the first stitch under the LH needle, from the front to the back, or knitwise.

Always hold the yarn with the RH.

2 With the right hand, wrap the yarn around the RH needle tip from front to back and tighten it gently, so that the yarn slides between the tips of the LH and RH needles.

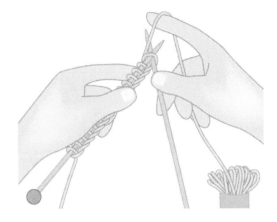

3 With the tip of the RH needle, bring the yarn toward you through the stitch on the LH needle, creating a new loop on the RH needle.

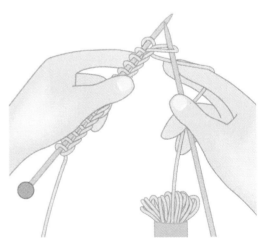

4 Slide the RH needle over the tip of the LH needle so the stitch you just worked ends up on the RH needle. With the RH, gently tighten the yarn on the RH needle.

6 When there are no more stitches on the LH needle, the first row is finished. Switch needles: hold the empty needle in the RH and the needle with all the stitches in the LH. You are now ready for the next row.

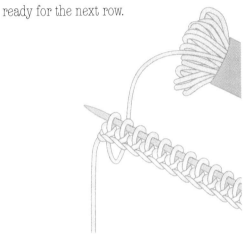

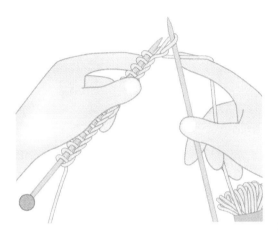

5 Repeat steps 1 to 4: as you work, the row grows on the RH needle and the number of stitches decreases on the LH needle.

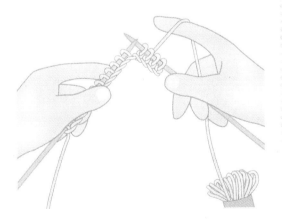

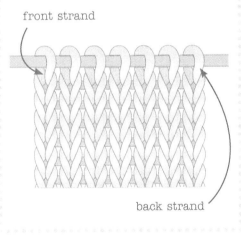

front strand

back strand

The Purl Stitch

Once you master both the knit stitch and the purl stitch, you will be able to combine the two to produce many different stitch patterns (see pages 18-23.)

1 Hold the needle with the cast on stitches (or the preceding rows) in the LH. Hold the yarn in front of the work. Insert the RH needle behind the front strand of the first stitch, or purlwise, under the LH needle.

2 With the right hand, bring the yarn over and around the RH needle tip from front to back and tighten gently so the yarn goes between the tips of the needles.

3 With the tip of the RH needle, bring the yarn through the stitch on the LH needle, creating a new loop on the RH needle.

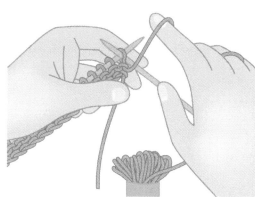

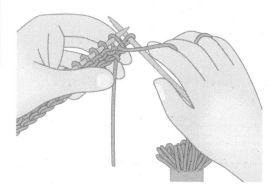

4 Slide the RH needle toward the tip of the LH needle so that the stitch is on the RH needle only. With the RH, gently tighten the yarn on the RH needle.

6 When there are no more stitches on the LH needle, the row is finished. Switch needles; take the empty needle in the RH and hold the needle with all the stitches in the LH. Ready for the next row!

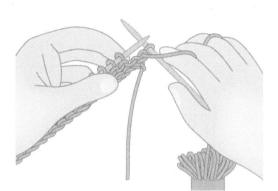

5 Repeat steps 1-4: as you work, the row grows on the RH needle and the number of stitches decreases on the LH needle.

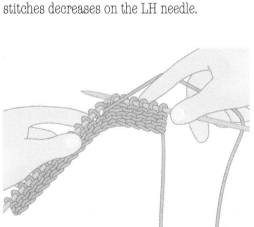

Tips

Adding New Yarn

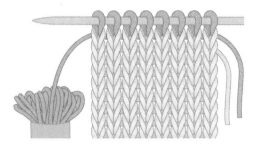

If you don't have enough yarn for a new row or if you're changing color in the next row, leave the old yarn on the edge of the work and knit the next row with the new yarn. Leave a tail about 6 inches long, so you can weave it in when finishing the project.

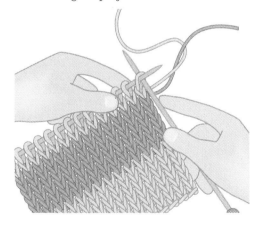

When creating stripes, don't cut the yarn you are not using at the moment, as you can pick it up later. If the stripes are wide, cross the different color yarn every other row.

Fixing a Dropped Stitch

When you see a horizontal strand of yarn in your project, it is a dropped stitch. If you dropped several stitches, start from the lowest row and work your way up to the current one.

A Knit Stitch

The dropped stitch is in the front of the work. From the front, insert a crochet hook into the stitch and hook the horizontal strand of yarn. Pull the strand through the loop on the hook to repair the dropped stitch.

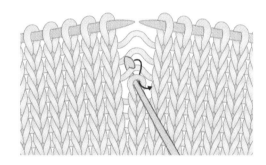

A Purl Stitch

The dropped stitch is in the back of the work. From the back, insert a crochet hook into the stitch and hook the horizontal strand of yarn. Pull the strand through the loop on the hook to repair the dropped stitch.

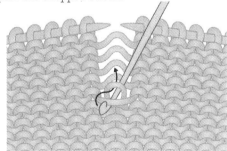

Binding Off

When your project is finished, it is important to bind off (BO) the stitches so the project doesn't unravel. Contrary to popular belief, this technique is not more difficult than casting on.

1 Hold the needles just like you would for a new row. Knit the first two stitches.

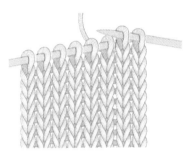

2 Insert the tip of the LH needle into the first stitch on the RH needle, which is further away. Pull the first stitch to pass it over the second stitch. There is now only one stitch left on the RH needle.

3 Knit a new stitch from the LH needle, so that there are once again two stitches on the RH needle.

4 Repeat steps 2 and 3 until there is only one stitch left on the RH needle. Cut the yarn, leaving a tail about 6" (15cm) long. Gently pull the RH needle to make the stitch looser. Insert the end of the yarn into the stitch and pull on the yarn to fasten off the stitch.

The projects in this book are bound off by a row of knit stitches, but depending on the desired effect, it is possible to purl the bind-off row using the same method —simply purl the stitches in the row rather than knitting them, but pass them over in the same way.

Mixing Stitches

Combine knitting and purling to make different stitch patterns. Simple!

❶ Garter Stitch

Exclusively knit rows. As a result, the same undulations are formed on each side, making this stitch reversible and quite dense. To count the number of rows, add the rows of waves to the rows of dips between them.

> Row 1 and all the other rows:
> Knit every stitch.

❷ Stockinette Stitch

Alternate a knit row on the right side (RS) of your project and a purl row on the wrong side (WS) of your project. The knit row creates a V shape; the purl row creates a wavy pattern. To find the number of rows, count either the number of V's on one side, or the number of waves on the other side.

Stockinette stitch tends to curl up at the edges. To flatten it, you can use garter stitch, seed stitch, or ribbing at the beginning and end of each row.

> Row 1 and all odd rows:
> Knit every stitch.
> Row 2 and all even rows:
> Purl every stitch.

❸ Reverse Stockinette Stitch

Work exactly like stockinette stitch, but reverse the sides.

> Row 1 and all odd rows:
> Purl every stitch.
> Row 2 and all even rows:
> Knit every stitch.

❹ Stockinette stitch with stripes in reverse stockinette stitch

Alternate 3 knit rows and 1 purl row.

> Row 1: Knit every stitch.
> Row 2: Purl every stitch.
> Row 3: Knit every stitch.
> Row 4: Knit every stitch.
> Repeat these 4 rows.

The word "selvage" or "selvedge" is used for the right and the left edges of your work. If a pattern includes selvage stitches, the first stitch of each row is slipped on the RH needle without being knitted or always knitted (knit stitch), as is the case in this book.

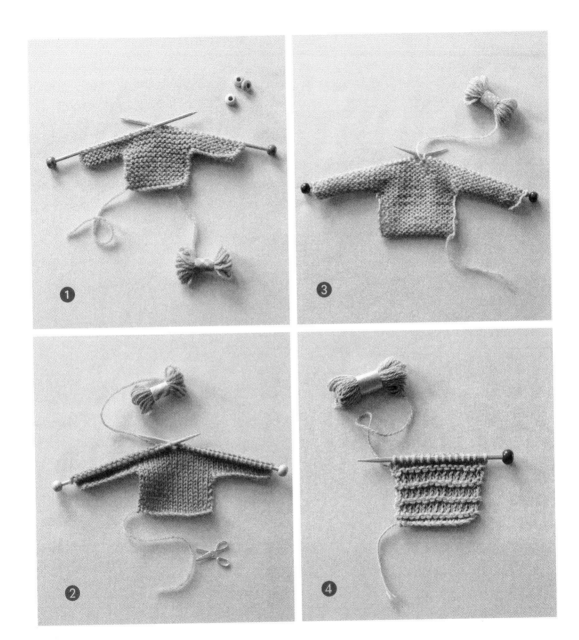

⑤ Seed Stitch

Seed stitch consists of rows of alternating knit and purl stitches. Stitches that are knitted on one row will be purled on the next; stitches that are purled on one row will be knitted on the next. To make things easier, the pattern as written has an odd number of stitches, so each row starts with the same stitch.

With an odd number of stitches:
All rows:
Knit 1, purl 1. Repeat until end of row.

⑥ Moss Stitch

Moss stitch is a variation of seed stitch. Rather than alternating every row, stitches that are knitted on one row will be knitted again on the next row before being purled on the following row. Stitches that are purled on one row will be purled again on the next row before being knitted on the following row. This creates taller "seeds" than the traditional seed stitch.

With an even number of stitches:
Rows 1 and 3: Knit 1, purl 1. Repeat until end of row.
Rows 2 and 4: Purl 1, knit 1. Repeat until end of row.
Repeat these 4 rows as established.

⑦ Basket Weave Stitch

In this checkered pattern, each box represents 3 stitches and 4 rows.

With multiples of 6 stitches +3:
Row 1: Knit 3, purl 3. Repeat until 3 stitches remain, knit 3.
Row 2: Purl 3, knit 3. Repeat until 3 stitches remain, purl 3.
Rows 3 and 4: Repeat rows 1 and 2.
Row 5: Purl 3, knit 3. Repeat until 3 stitches remain, purl 3.
Row 6: Knit 3, purl 3. Repeat until 3 stitches remain, knit 3.
Rows 7 and 8: Repeat rows 5 and 6.
Repeat these 8 rows as established.

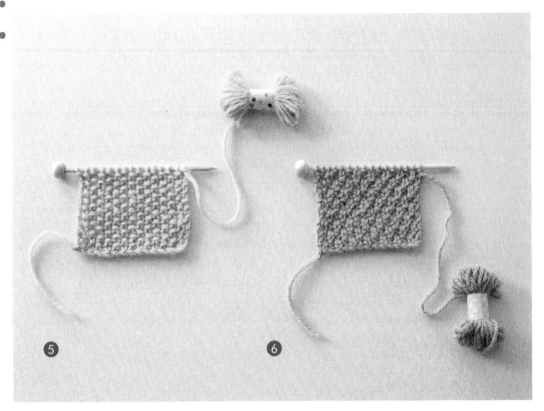

Ribbing

Ribbing is formed by alternated knit and purl stitches to create vertical ribs. They are commonly used for the wrists of sleeves, the bottom of sweaters, and the border of hats or scarves because the pattern is reversible and is stretchy.

❽ 1x1 ribbing

With an even number of stitches:
All rows: Knit 1, purl 1. Repeat until end of row.

❾ 2x2 ribbing

With a multiple of 4 stitches + 2
Row 1 and all odd rows: Knit 2, purl 2. Repeat until 2 stitches remain, knit 2.
Row 2 and all even rows: Purl 2, knit 2. Repeat until 2 stitches remain, purl 2.

Alternating stripes

Stockinette stitch is perfect for playing with color!
To introduce a new yarn color, see page 16.

❿ Thin stripes with three colors

Working with three different colors of yarn, change color at the start of each row. Because you are working with an odd number of colors, the working yarn should always be on the correct side of the project, and you can continue the pattern indefinitely.

Working in Stockinette Stitch:

Cast on and work Row 1 with Color A.
Row 2: Attach Color B and work to end of row.
Row 3: Attach Color C and work to end of row.
Row 4: Pick up Color A and work to end of row.
Row 5: Pick up Color B and work to end of row.
Row 6: Pick up Color C and work to end of row.
Repeat stripe pattern as established.

⓫ Two- or four-row stripes

If your stripes are not too wide, you won't need to cut the yarn—simply carry the yarn up the side of your work.

Work wider stripes in the same manner as the thin stripes—simply work multiple even rows of each color.

To bind off rib stitches, it is better to knit them as they present themselves (i.e. knit a knit, purl a purl), before sliding the preceding stitch over it.

Increasing and Decreasing

By adding or subtracting one or more stitches, you can modify the shape of your project.

Decreasing

2 stitches together

This is the simplest method.

Knit 2 together (k2tog)

Insert the RH needle into the first 2 stitches (sts) from left to right. Knit them together as if they were one stitch.

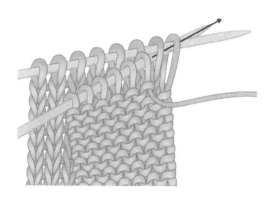

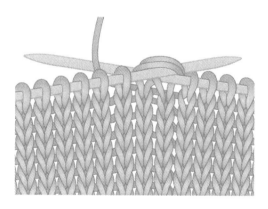

Purl 2 together (p2tog)

Insert the RH needle into the first 2 sts from right to left. Purl them together as if they were one stitch.

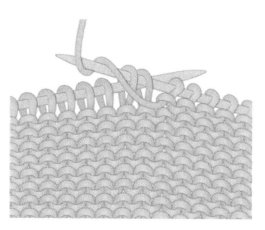

Slip 1, knit 1, pass slipped stitch over (s1, k1, psso *or* SKP)

1 Slip the first stitch from the LH needle onto the RH needle without knitting it.

2 Knit the next stitch. Pass the slipped stitch over the knitted stitch on the RH needle.

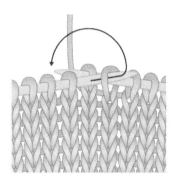

SKP results in a left-leaning decrease, while k2tog results in a right-leaning decrease. The two decreases are often used on either side of a pattern for symmetry.

Increasing

There are several methods for increasing stitches. The projects offered in this book call for the most inconspicuous method—make 1 (m1).

1 Insert the RH needle from front to back into the space between the stitches on the RH and LH needles. Gently pull the strand of yarn between these stitches and place the resulting loop on the LH needle.

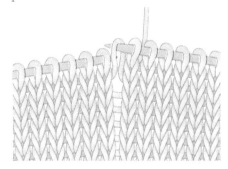

2 Insert the tip of the RH needle from front to back in this new loop and knit it as you would a regular stitch. This will twist the loop and create a stitch that blends in seamlessly with your work.

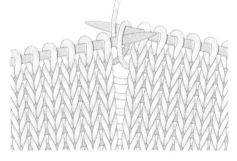

Finishing

Weaving in Loose Ends

With a tapestry needle, weave the loose end of the yarn under a few stitches on the WS of the work before cutting it. If there is just one end, you can do this along the edge of the work.

If several loose ends need to be finished, they can be woven horizontally across the work.

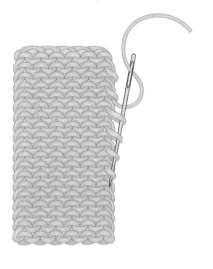

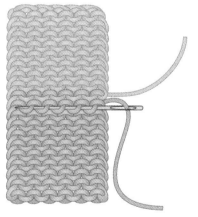

Seaming

Seaming Edges

Lay the two pieces flat, next to each other, with the RS facing up. Starting from the bottom-left corner of the right-hand piece, insert a tapestry needle between the first and second stitch.

Then, insert the needle between the first and second stitch on the bottom-right corner of the left-hand piece. Pull this establishing stitch snugly.

Alternating between the LH and RH piece, continue to sew stitches between the first and second stitches from the edges, going up two rows at a time. This will create a neat, zig-zag stitch at the seam.

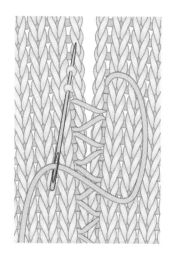

Seaming cast-on (CO) or bind-off (BO) rows

Lay the two pieces flat, one above the other, with the RS facing up, so that the stitches of each piece line up with one another.

Insert a tapestry needle under the first stitch at the bottom-left edge of the top piece. Then insert the needle under the first stitch at the top-right edge of the bottom piece. Pull the yarn snugly. As you continue seaming the pieces in this manner, your seam will mimic the appearance of a knit row.

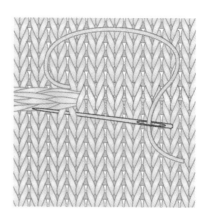

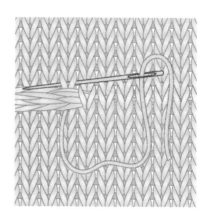

Button Loops

1 Determine where you would like the button loop to be. Insert a tapestry needle at this location from the WS, pulling the yarn through to the front of the work and securing the end on the WS. Reinsert the needle from the front of the work where you'd like the loop to end, and adjust the resulting loop so that it's the correct width for your button.

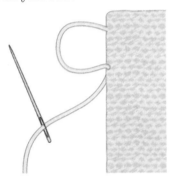

2 To finish the button loop, insert the needle into the loop, then over the working yarn. Gently pull and slide this first stitch to the beginning of the button loop. Repeat this step all around the loop and fasten off on the WS of your work.

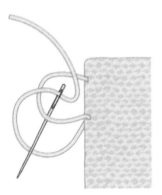

Fringe

1 Cut strands of yarn twice as long as you want the fringe to be plus ½ inch. Take your desired number of strands and fold them in half. Insert a crochet hook from back to front into the stitch where you'd like to attach the fringe. Hook the fringe strands at the fold you created and gently pull them through the stitch.

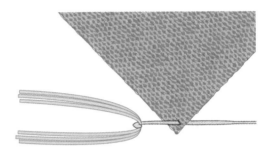

2 Insert the two ends of the fringe into the resulting loop and pull snugly to close the loop and secure the fringe on the piece.

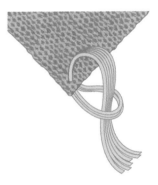

3 Repeat these two steps wherever you would like fringe on your piece. Trim the fringe evenly after attaching all of the fringe to your piece.

Pompoms

1 With a compass, trace two identical circles with identical holes in the middle on medium-strength cardboard (for example, a large circle 1½"/4cm in diameter with a ½"/1cm hole in the middle.) Cut out the two circles and their holes, and put the two resulting doughnut-shaped pieces on top of each other.

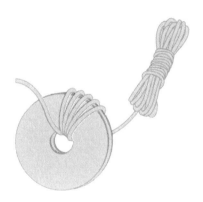

2 Thread a tapestry needle with yarn. Starting from the hole, wrap the yarn around the two doughnut pieces, working in a circle until there is no room left in the hole.

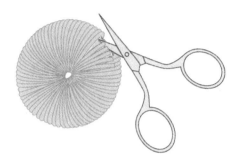

3 Insert a scissor blade between the edges of the two doughnuts and cut the yarn along the outside rim. This will separate the doughnuts —do not pull them apart yet.

4 Wrap another strand of yarn between the two doughnuts, around the yarn inside, pull it as tightly as possible, and knot it securely. Gently remove the cardboard doughnuts. Fluff and trim the pompom so that it is circular and even.

Pretty Bows

Worked entirely in knit stitches, these jewels are quick and easy to create! Mirror, mirror, on the wall, who will be the fairest of them all?

Materials

For both projects:
- Sport or DK weight yarn in the colors of your choice
- Lurex yarn in black or metallic (optional)
- Size 4 (3.5mm) knitting needles
- Tapestry needle
- Sewing needle
- Sewing thread that matches the color of your yarn

For the necklace:
- Chain, about 20" (35cm) long
- 1 lobster claw clasp
- 3 oval split rings
- Jewelry pliers (to open and close the split rings)

For the bracelet:
- 1 snap

❸ Find the center of the rectangle. Cut a length of yarn and wrap it tightly around the center-point to create the bow. Tie off and secure the yarn on the WS of the bow. Weave in all the ends.

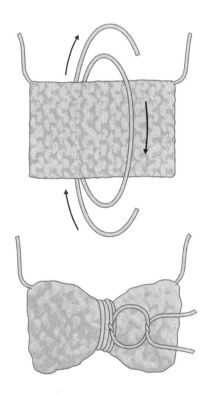

❶ Small bow: Cast on 5 sts and knit 14 rows. Large bow: Cast on 8 sts and knit 22 rows.

❷ Bind off. The side that shows the BO ridge is the WS.

The size of the yarn and needles is given as an example. The important thing is that the knitting be dense enough to retain its shape. For more of a jewel look, mix regular yarn and shiny Lurex yarn.

Necklace

Create a small bow.

Cut the chain into two equal parts. Attach a split ring to one end of each chain piece. Then, insert each ring between two stitches on either side of the bow. Close the split rings so the bow is attached to the chain. At the other end of one piece of chain, attach another split ring. At the end of the other piece of chain, attach the lobster claw.

Headband

Create a large bow.

With another yarn color, cast on 4 sts, leaving a long tail. Knit a long enough strip to fit snugly around your head. Bind off. Weave in the ends. With the sewing needle and thread, sew the bow on one side of the headband.

Bracelet

Create a large bow.

With another yarn color, cast on 4 sts and knit a strip long enough to fit snugly around your wrist. Bind off. Weave in the ends.

With the sewing needle and thread, sew one side of the snap to the RS of one end of the strip. Sew the other side of the snap to the WS of the other end of the strip. Sew the bow onto the center of the strip.

Pouches and More ...

You can keep your coins and small treasures in colorful small pouches. Add a charm to identify each pouch!

Materials
- Sport or DK weight yarn in the colors of your choice
- Size 4 (3.5mm) and 6 (4.0mm) knitting needles
- Tapestry needle
- Buttons
- Sewing thread that matches the color of your yarn
- Sewing needle
- Metal studs and scraps of felt
- Key ring and cell phone strap
- Ribbons
- Beads
- Synthetic or cotton filling

Pouch
(Finished model: 6 x 5" = 15 x 12cm)

Flap
Cast on 15 sts using size 6 needles.
Rows 1 and 2: Knit all sts.
Rows 3, 5, 7, 9 and 11: Knit 2, make 1, knit to last 2 sts, make 1, knit 2—25 sts at end of row 11.
Rows 4, 6, 8, 10 and 12: Knit 2, purl to last 2 sts, knit 2.
Rows 13 and 15: Knit all sts.
Rows 14 and 16: Knit 2, purl to last 2 sts, knit 2.

Back
Work 26 rows in stockinette stitch.

Front
Work 25 rows in stockinette stitch.
Bind off.

Pink Flap Pouch

Flap
Following the pattern on the previous page, work the 16 rows for the flap in pink.

Back
Work the 26 rows for the back in alternating gray and yellow stripes.

Front
*Work the 25 rows for the front continuing the gray and yellow stripe pattern.
Bind off.*

Yellow Flap Pouch

Flap
Following the pattern on the previous page, work the 16 rows for the flap in yellow.

Back
Work the 26 rows for the back in gray.

Front
Work the 25 rows for the front in this stripe sequence: 2 rows gray, 4 rows pink, 2 rows yellow, 4 rows green, 13 rows gray. Bind off.

Coin Purse
(Finished model: 3½ x 3" = 9 x 8cm)

Flap
Cast on 9 sts using size 6 needle.
Rows 1 and 2: Knit all sts.
Rows 3, 5, 7 and 9: Knit 2, make 1, knit to last 2 sts, make 1, knit 2—17 sts at end of row 9.
Rows 4, 6, 8 and 10: Knit 2, purl to last 2 sts, knit 2.
Rows 11 and 13: Knit all sts.
Rows 12 and 14: Knit 2, purl to last 2 sts, knit 2.

Back
Work in stockinette stitch for 18 rows.

Front
Work in stockinette stitch for 17 rows.
Bind off purlwise.

Flap
Following the pattern, work 14 rows in green.

Back
Work the 18 rows for the back in the following stripe pattern:
2 rows pink
4 rows yellow

Front
Work the 17 rows for the front continuing the stripe pattern from the back.
Bind off.

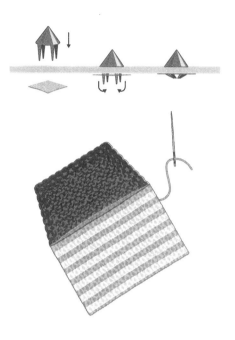

Finishing

Weave in loose ends. Fold the pouch so that the widest part of the flap aligns with the bottom edge of the piece and sew the sides. Make a button loop on each side or in the middle of the flap and sew the button(s) on the front of the pouch to match these loops.

Add the metal studs at regular intervals. To secure them, place a small square of felt on the WS of the piece before inserting the stud and pressing the prongs in. Trim the felt if necessary.

Pyramid Key Chain

① Cast on 12 sts using size 4 needles. Beginning with a purl row, work 8 rows of stockinette stitch, changing color every row. Bind off, leaving a long tail for assembling the piece.

② **Note:** Follow the diagram for assembly. Fold the piece in half vertically, so that the two halves of the BO edge sit on top of one another. Sew these halves together. At the CO edge, take both corners and fold them toward each other, so they meet at the center point. Sew these flaps down along the CO edge. Tuck the ends into the pocket you have created, add a small amount of filling, and sew the remaining hole closed.

③ Attach a cell phone strap to one of the pyramid's points and attach the strap to a key ring. Fold two 8" (20cm) ribbons around the key ring and use a metal stud to secure them in place. Attach a bead to the key ring with additional yarn.

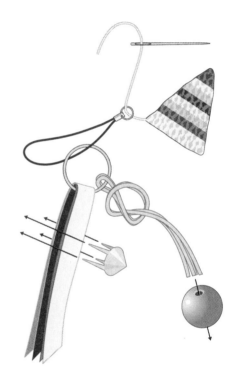

Variation
The larger pyramid calls for 20 sts and a change of color every 2 rows. Bind off after 12 rows.

Owls

These fun little birds can change in size with the weight of the yarn used or number of stitches or rows worked.

Finishing

❶ Fold the body in half horizontally. Shape the ears by weaving the yarn along a few stitches on the inside, so they are not visible on the RS. Pull gently to pucker the work and form the ears. (See illustration). Tuck wings between the two halves of the body before sewing the sides shut, anchoring the wings in place.

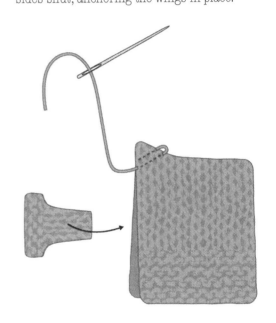

Body

Cast on 12 sts.
Rows 1–10: Work in garter stitch.
Rows 11–28: Work in stockinette stitch.
Rows 29–39: Work in garter stitch.
Bind off.

Wings (Make 2)

Cast on 8 sts.
Rows 1 and 2: Knit all sts.
Row 3: K2tog 4 times—4 sts.
Row 4: Purl all sts.
Row 5: Knit all sts.
Bind off.

2 Tuck ends into the inside of the body and insert the filling. Sew the bottom closed, fasten off, and weave in the last end.

3 Take a 1–1¼" (1.5 cm to 2 cm) square of felt to make the beak. Fold it in two and center it on the head of the owl. Sew along the long side of the beak to secure it to the owl. Sew the buttons for eyes.

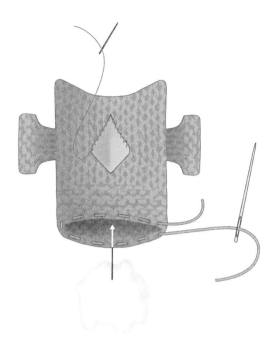

Egg Cozies

Create nice knitted hats for your eggs! They will stay nice and warm for you to enjoy!

Materials
- Sport or DK weight wool yarn in colors of your choice
- Size 4 (3.5mm) knitting needles
- Tapestry needle

For the hats
- Light cardboard, 1 x 4" (2 x 10cm)

For the scarves
- Size B (2.25mm) crochet hook

WS of the piece.
The last row of decreases is done on the WS

Hat

Note: Change colors as you like to make stripes.
Cast on 30 sts.

Rows 1 and 2: Work in garter stitch.

Rows 3–13: Work in stockinette stitch.

Row 14: P2tog 15 times—15 sts.

Row 15: K2tog 7 times. Knit last stitch—8 sts.

Row 16: P2tog 4 times—4 sts.

To bind off: Slip the sts off the RH needle without knitting them. Cut the yarn, leaving a long tail, and thread the yarn onto a tapestry needle. Pass the yarn through the 4 stitches. Gently pull and pass it through a second time so the bind off is secure.

Finishing

Sew the hat with the ends of the different colors used while knitting and weave in the ends. Make a little tassel and sew to the top (see instructions on next page).

Variation: A or C

Starting with row 7, change colors every two rows.

Variation: B

Row 7: Dark green
Rows 8–10: Light pink
Rows 11–12: Light green (until the end)

Variation: D

Row 7: Light green
Rows 8–9: Orange
Row 10: Light green
Rows 11–12: Light pink
Work in light green until the end.

Small Tassel

① Fold the light cardboard rectangle in half. Take 3 pieces of yarn together and wrap them around the rectangle 10 times.

③ With another color, tie all the strands of yarn together a little farther down from the first knot. Tuck the ends into the tassel.

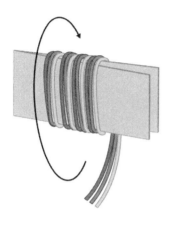

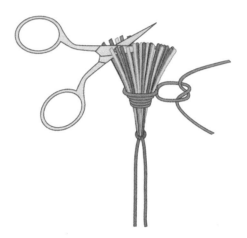

② With the same color yarn as the top of the hat and a tapestry needle, tie the strands on one end of the tassel together. Slip the tassel off the cardboard.

④ Cut the other end of the tassel. Using the ends of the yarn that match the top of the hat, secure the tassel to the hat.

Scarf

Cast on 5 sts.
Work in garter stitch for 6½" (18cm).
Bind off. Weave in ends. Attach 5 pieces of fringe at each end and trim them to about ¾" (1.5cm).

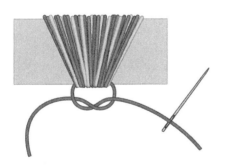

Tea Time

To keep your tea hot and protect your table, why not create colorful coasters and mug sleeves in a jiffy?

Materials

- Worsted weight yarn in colors of your choosing
- Size 7 (4.5mm) and 8 (5.0mm) knitting needles
- Tapestry needle
- Buttons
- Sewing thread that matches the color of your yarn
- Sewing needle

Coaster

Cast on 21 stitches using size 8 needles.

First edge
Rows 1 to 4: Work in seed stitch.

Middle section
Row 5: Knit 1, purl 1, knit 1, purl 15, knit 1, purl 1, knit 1.
Row 6: Knit 1, purl 1, knit 17, purl 1, knit 1.
Rows 7–25: Repeat rows 5 and 6 nine times. Repeat row 5 once more.

Last edge
Rows 26–29: Repeat rows 1–4.
Bind off.
Weave in ends.

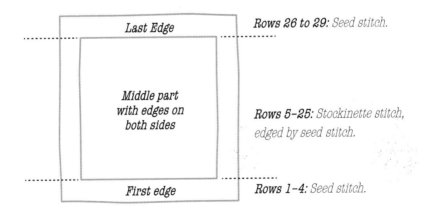

Last Edge

Middle part with edges on both sides

First edge

Rows 26 to 29: Seed stitch.

Rows 5-25: Stockinette stitch, edged by seed stitch.

Rows 1-4: Seed stitch.

Mug Sleeves

Using size 7 needles, cast on 50 sts.

Note: Depending on the size of your mug, it might be necessary to modify the number of cast on stitches—check the fit after a few rows. If you modify your cast on, make sure you are casting on an even number of stitches.

Rows 1 and 2: Knit 1, purl 1.

Rows 3 and 4: Purl 1, knit 1.

Repeat these 4 rows until the sleeve is tall enough to cover your mug, ending on row 1 or 3.

Bind off knitwise.

Weave in ends.

Variation: Coral

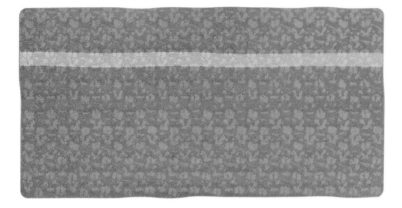

Finish with moss stitch in coral.

2 rows garter stitch in light coral.

18 rows moss stitch in coral.

Cast on row.

Variation: Light Coral and Yellow

Moss stitch beginning row 1 or 3, depending on the last row worked.

Moss stitch ending with row 2 or 4.

Cast on row.

Finishing

On one short side of the rectangle, create 3 button loops, being mindful of the mug handle of course! On the other short side, sew the buttons so they align with the loops.

Pretty Hearts

Knitted by hand they become quite a declaration…

Materials
- DK weight wool yarn in colors of your choosing
- Mohair yarn (optional)
- Size 4 (3.5mm) and 6 (4.0mm) knitting needles
- Tapestry needle
- Safety pins
- Sewing thread that matches the color of your yarn
- Sewing needle

Each heart is worked in garter stitch. The little heart requires size 4 needles and wool yarn in a solid color. The large heart requires size 6 needles and 2 strands of yarn (or one wool and one mohair) held together.

First Lobe
Cast on 4 sts.

Rows 1 and 2: Knit all sts.

Row 3: Knit 1, make 1, knit 2, make 1, knit 1 —6 sts.

Row 4: Knit all sts.

Row 5: Knit 1, make 1, knit 4, make 1, knit 1 —8 sts.

Rows 6–8: Knit all sts. Cut the yarn, leaving a long tail. Push the lobe to the far end of your knitting needle.

Second Lobe
Work the same as the first lobe, working while keeping the first lobe on your needle.

Do not cut the yarn at the end of the second lobe.

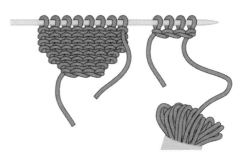

Tip of the Heart
Row 9: Knit the 8 sts of the second lobe, then the 8 sts of the first lobe, being mindful not to leave a space between the two. Gently pull on the tail from the first lobe to make sure that it does not come undone—16 sts.

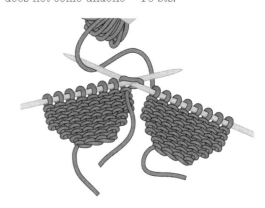

Row 10 and all even rows: Knit all sts.

Row 11: Knit 1, SKP, knit 10, k2tog, knit 1
—14 sts.
Row 13: Knit 1, SKP, knit 8, k2tog, knit 1
—12 sts.
Row 15: Knit 1, SKP, knit 6, k2tog, knit 1
—10 sts.
Row 17: Knit 1, SKP, knit 4, k2tog, knit 1
—8 sts.
Row 19: Knit 1, SKP, knit 2, k2tog, knit 1
—6 sts.
Row 21: Knit 1, SKP, k2tog, knit 1—4 sts.
Row 23: SKP, k2tog—2 sts.
Row 24: SKP. Cut the yarn and pass it through
the last stitch to fasten off.

Finishing
Weave in the ends. Sew a brooch pin on the back
of the heart, or sew the heart directly onto a
piece of clothing or an accessory.

*You can sew hearts
on your sweaters to
customize them—large ones as
elbow patches, small ones to
hide a hole, or at random to
put you in a good mood!*

Soft Jewelry

Transform your yarn scraps into attractive jewelry!

Materials
- Fingering or sport weight yarn in colors of your choosing
- Lurex yarn
- Size 3 (3.25mm) or 4 (3.5mm) needles, depending on the weight of your yarn
- Sewing thread that matches the color of your yarn
- Sewing needle
- Wood bracelets (craft shops) or plastic bangles
- Chain
- Split rings
- Clasp
- Jewelry pliers

Preparation
Lurex yarn is generally too thin for size 3 or 4 needles. Prepare a ball of yarn with two strands of Lurex yarn held together.

Bracelet

Directions
For a bracelet that's 1" (3cm) wide and 3¼" (8cm) in diameter, cast on 16 sts.

Work in stockinette stitch for 80 rows.

Note: The number of stitches cast on and rows worked will depend on the bracelet you are using. Check the fit as you go.

For your first bracelet project, it is better to knit irregular stripes or with a solid color, both of which allow you to stop when the strip is long enough without disrupting a pattern.

Finishing
Weave in the ends. Fold the strip in half width-wise and sew the CO and BO edges together to create a tube. Slip it over the bracelet and fold back the open edges. With a sewing needle and thread, sew the edges closed, matching any stripes. Position the seam on the inside of the bracelet so it is not visible when worn.

When knitting yarn bracelets, it is important to use smaller knitting needles than the ones recommended on the yarn band—1 or 2 sizes smaller—so the knitting is thick enough to maintain its shape.

Confetti

Work in garter stitch.

Cast on 4 sts.
Rows 1 and 2: Knit all sts.
Row 3: Knit 1, make 1, knit 2, make 1, knit 1 —6 sts.
Row 4: Knit all sts.
Row 5: Knit 1, make 1, knit 4, make 1, knit 1 —8 sts.
Rows 6-10: Knit all sts.
Row 11: Knit 1, SKP, knit 2, k2tog, knit 1 —6 sts.
Row 12: Knit all.
Row 13: Knit 1, SKP, k2tog, knit 1 —4 sts.
Row 14: Bind off, slipping the first stitch without knitting it, as for an SKP.

Finishing

Choose which side will be the RS of the confetti and weave in the ends on the WS.

Necklace

Knit an odd number of confetti [about 11 for a 28" (70cm) necklace]. Choose where to place each piece of confetti on the necklace. Attach one in the middle of the chain with a split ring. Attach the others on either side of the middle one, about 1¼" (3cm) apart. Finish by attaching split rings to both ends of the chain. Attach the clasp to one of the rings.

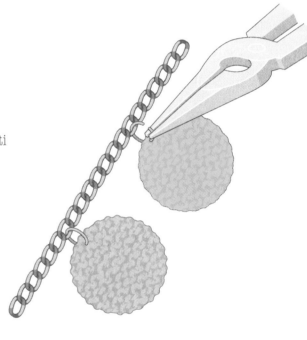

My Collection of Scarves

A scarf is generally the first piece made by a knitter. In order to knit without getting bored, I suggest knitting a scarf that is neither too long nor too wide—or you can use a very thick yarn! You can make a whole collection of scarves in no time.

Materials

Dark Pink Scarf
- One .88oz/25g ball of mohair/silk yarn
- Size 4 (3.5mm) knitting needles

Purple Scarf
- Two 1.75oz/50g balls of worsted weight wool blend yarn
- Size 8 (5.0mm) knitting needles

Pink Scarf with Fringe
- Three 1.75oz/50g balls of DK weight wool blend yarn
- Size 7 (4.5mm) knitting needles
- Piece of light cardboard 6" (14cm) wide
- Size D (3.25mm) or E (3.5mm) crochet hook

Light Blue Scarf
- Two 3.5oz/100g balls of super-bulky wool yarn
- Size 13 (9.0mm) knitting needles

For all the scarves
- Tapestry needle

Dark Pink Scarf

Cast on 35 sts [for about 6" (15cm) width].
Work in garter stitch until you reach your desired length, or until you are left with about 12" (30cm) of yarn.
Bind off loosely.
Weave in ends.
Voila!

Purple Scarf

Cast on 26 sts [for about 6½" (16cm) width].
Rows 1–6: Work in garter stitch.
Row 7 and all odd rows (RS of the scarf): Knit all sts.
Row 8 and all even rows (WS of the scarf): Knit 4, purl 18, knit 4.
When the second ball is almost finished, after an even row, work 6 rows in garter stitch.
Bind off loosely.
Weave in ends.

The quantity and type of yarn used is given as a suggestion only.

Pink Scarf with Fringe

Cast on 33 sts [for about 6" (16cm) width].

Note: The number of stitches can be modified, but it is important that the total be an odd number. Work in seed stitch, starting each row with a knit stitch.

When the scarf is a little over 3 feet (1m) long, bind off loosely.

Weave in ends.

Finishing

For the fringe, cut 11" (28cm) pieces of yarn. Working with 3 strands held together (see p. 28), attach the fringe at even intervals at both ends of the scarf.

Light Blue Scarf

Cast on 20 sts [for about 8" (20cm) width].

Note: The stitch chosen for this scarf will curl up at the edges, so it will seem a little narrower.

Rows 1–3: Knit all sts.
Row 4: Purl all sts.
Repeat rows 1–4 until you reach your desired length.
Repeat rows 1–3.
Bind off (on RS of the piece).
Weave in ends.

You are the designer! Create your own trademark by sewing a charm or a label onto your pieces.

To create a customized scarf, first determine its width. 6 to 8 inches (15 to 20cm) is a traditional width, but you can add more stitches if you want to create a long and wide wrap! Then, figure out the number of stitches to cast on by using the gauge listed on the ball band, or better yet, a sample swatch that you have knit (see page 62).

To learn how to incorporate a new ball of yarn, see page 16.

Basic Knitted Hat

A pretty knitted hat will make heads turn! The decreases create an interesting pattern on top. The same principle can be adapted for different hats depending on the number of stitches and the thickness of the yarn.

Materials

- Two 1.75oz/50g balls of worsted weight, multicolored yarn
- Size 8 (5.0mm) knitting needles
- Tapestry needle
- Light cardboard and compass

The ribbing (see page 22) prevents the knitted hat from curling up and creates some elasticity in the border, keeping the hat in place.

Ribbing

Cast on 90 sts (for a head circumference of 22" (54cm).

Row 1-8: Work in 1x1 or 2x2 ribbing, depending on your preference.

Continue in stockinette stitch for 18 rows, or until your work measures 5" (12cm). The length of the hat can be modified, as long as you work an even number of rows.

Top of the hat

Row 1: Knit 8, k2tog. Repeat until the end of the row—81 sts.

Row 2 and all even rows: Purl all sts.

Row 3: Knit 7, k2tog. Repeat until the end of the row—72 sts.

Row 5: Knit 6, k2tog. Repeat until the end of the row—63 sts.

Following odd rows: Knit 1 stitch less before the k2tog. Repeat until the end of the row.

Row 15: Knit 1, k2tog. Repeat until the end of the row—18 sts.

Row 17: K2tog. Repeat until the end of the row —9 sts.

Binding off the stitches

After the last decrease row, slide the stitches off the LH needle without knitting them. Cut the yarn, leaving a long tail, and thread it onto a tapestry needle. Pass the yarn through the 9 remaining stitches, pull snugly, and pass the yarn through the stitches again to secure the end of the piece (see page 40).

Finishing

Sew the hat from bottom to top. Weave in ends. Create a small 1½" (4cm) pompom (see page 29) and sew it to the top of the hat.

To create a wool hat for yourself, first measure the circumference of your head. Based on the swatch (see page 62) or the number of stitches indicated on the ball band, determine the number of stitches needed to cast on. Round up so the decreases are regularly spaced on the top of the hat. For example, if you choose 87 stitches, cast on 90, which will be divided into 9 sections of 10 stitches.

In this example, 2x2 ribbing is ideal as it will be regularly spaced as well.

Elegant Wool Hat

A retro-inspired design, or how to be trendy when it is freezing out!

Body of the Hat

Cast on 50 sts [for a head circumference of 22" (54cm)].

Work in garter stitch until work measures 5" (13cm).

Top of the hat

Row 1: Knit 3, k2tog. Repeat until the end of the row—40 sts.

Row 2 and all following even rows: Purl all sts (WS).

Row 3: Knit 2, k2tog. Repeat until the end of the row—30 sts.

Row 5: Knit1, k2tog. Repeat until the end of the row—20 sts.

Row 7: K2tog. Repeat until the end of the row —10 sts.

Row 9: K2tog. Repeat until the end of the row—5 sts.

Binding off the stitches

Slide the stitches off the RH needle without knitting them. Cut the yarn, leaving a long tail, and thread it onto a tapestry needle. Pass the yarn through the 5 remaining stitches, pull snugly, and pass the yarn through the stitches again to secure the end of the piece (see page 40). Choose the side of the piece that will be the RS of the hat. (Since the hat was worked in garter stitch, it is reversible.)

Finishing

Sew the hat from bottom to top. Weave in ends.

Bow

Body of the bow

Cast on 10 sts.

Work rows 1–4 from Light Blue Scarf on page 56 six times.

Bind off loosely.

Central strip

Cast on 3 sts.

Work 3–3½" (8–9cm) in stockinette stitch.

Bind off.

Finishing

Weave in ends. Fold the center of the bow body to make an accordion. Secure with a few stitches using a needle and thread. Wrap the central strip around the fold and sew it on the back. Sew the bow onto the wool hat, or sew a safety pin on the back of the bow if you want to be able to take it off.

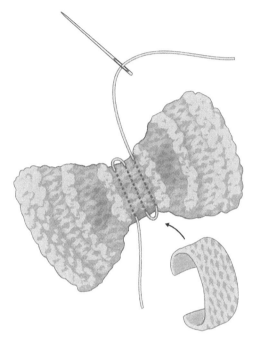

And a Few More Things...

Gauge Swatch

For a small piece, you can skip this step because it is easy to undo a few rows if the measurements seem off.

To follow a pattern or create a larger project, it is preferable to knit a swatch. It allows you to verify or establish the number of stitches you will need.

Using the information given on the ball band, cast on a few more stitches and knit a few more rows than called for. After knitting for a few inches, count the number of stitches and rows worked to measure 4" (10cm). It is helpful to mark these points in the swatch with pins.

If you are following a pattern

If the numbers obtained correspond to the gauge listed in the pattern, all is well!

If the numbers are a little over, it means your knitting style is looser, so you should use smaller knitting needles. If the numbers are a little under, use larger needles.

If you are creating a pattern

A simple calculation will suffice. For example, if you obtain 12 stitches for 4" (10cm) and you need to have a total width of 21" (52cm), figure out the number of stitches per inch and multiply by 21. In this case, cast on 63 stitches. The calculation will be the same for the number of rows, but it is not always necessary. Depending on the piece, you can adapt it or verify as you go.

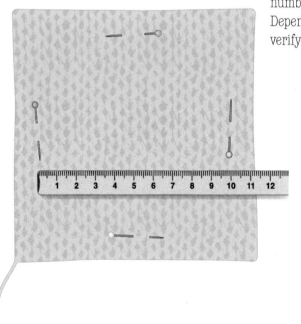

My Own Page

My favorite pattern!

....

The patterns that I love:

....

....

....

....

Create your own color scheme: